Go Mobile Now
Or Die

————————

Rateb "Rock" Shukoor

Acknowledgements

I would like to thank my family for their love and support, especially my parents, who gave up so much for us to be in the United States. I am 'still humbled' by what my mom and dad had to do in order for us to have a better life here. I also wanted to thank my wife, kids, brother and sisters who supported me through good and rough times. I also want to thank all of our team for sharing their insights and their willingness to collaborate with us to make every project a success. I do not believe in a one-man show and I would not have been here without the support of my team, family and friends. Thank you all for all you have done with me and for me.

Love,

— Rateb "Rock" Shukoor —

Do not read this book unless you are ready to take action!

Table of Contents

Introduction

*A*re you a business owner struggling with any of the following issues?

- Slower business growth
- Shrinking margins
- Increasing marketing costs
- Rising inventory costs

If you said yes to any of these, then you're at the right place.

We authored this book because we want to make a point very, very clear and send a wakeup call to business owners who are sitting on the sideline: if you aren't including mobile marketing in your strategic plan, odds are you won't be here in 12 to 18 months.

Think this is an exaggeration? Consider these facts:

- There are over 4.5 <u>billion</u> cell phones on the planet today: even some of the poorest villagers in remote parts of Africa have cell phones (there are more cell phones in the US than there are credit cards): it's estimated that over 500,000 cell phones are sold per day and this number is increasing

- By 2012, it's estimated that over 10 <u>trillion</u> text messages will be delivered (the average teen sends 2,272 messages per month: remember, the teen today is your consumer tomorrow)

- 1 in 5 US adult mobile phone owners have used their mobile device to make a purchase in the past month (Mobile Marketing Association & Luth Research, May 2010)

- 78% of business people use their mobile device to check their email (AT&T, March 2011)

- In most other industrialized nations especially in Europe and Asia, for years, consumers have been using their cell phones for handing all types of activities including paying bills, buying groceries and even paying for parking tickets

To further emphasize this trend, consider this graph from Morgan Stanley which shows that by approximately the year 2013, more people will access the Internet from a cell phone than from a desktop computer.

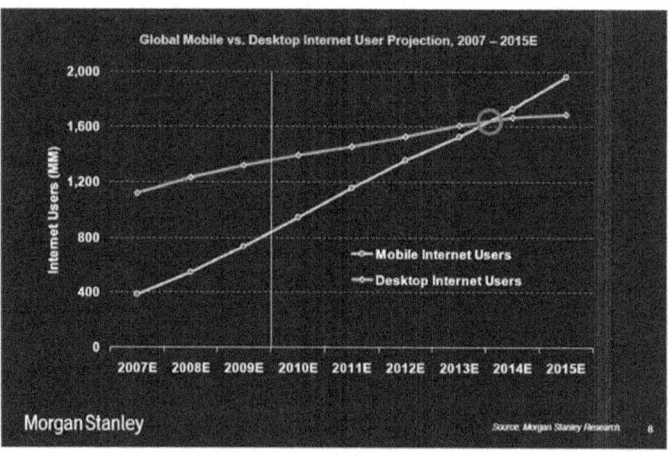

Internet access from mobile devices will exceed
access from desktop by the year 2013

The message is simple: **Go mobile now or die!**

That may sound alarmist to many of you, and we will explain why this is already true.

Scientists and sociologists are predicting that mobile phones will have a bigger impact on how we communicate as a society more than any communication device with maybe the exception of the printing press

Businesses that "get it" are enjoying enormous rewards (we will showcase multiple case studies throughout this book).

Mobile marketing enables your business to take control of its marketing and can help you grow even in a tough economy. This book contains specific strategies for using mobile marketing to grow your business and get customers today.

Businesses that "don't get it" risk being left behind (similar to what happened to companies in the travel and brokerage industries that refused to adapt and are no longer here).

There's an eloquent quote by General Eric Ken Shinseki: "If you don't like change, you're going to like irrelevancy even less."

Decide right now: do you plan on using this powerful new strategy to become a winner or do you want to get left behind and become irrelevant?

Let's get started.

Go Mobile Now or Die

Having spoken to thousands of business owners, a commonly phrased question is: "Is mobile marketing a fad?" Phrased another way: "Can I just ignore it and do what I've been doing?"

While nobody can predict the future, it's instructive to look at the previous major technological shift, the Internet revolution. This will provide some context why your business must go mobile immediately.

Prior to writing this book, we spent many years helping Fortune 500 companies reengineer their businesses to deal with rapidly changing market conditions. In the mid-1990s, as the Internet came on the scene, executives at traditional businesses (also known as brick and mortar companies) dismissed the Internet as a curiosity.

One very enterprising entrepreneur, Jeff Bezos, "got it" and decided to quit his high-paying hedge fund position to start what is now known as Amazon.com. Amazon.com enjoyed what is often referred to as the **first mover's advantage**, and many much larger companies that didn't "get it" ever managed to catch up, even with much larger budgets. In the tech industry, late-comers tend to pay for more and rarely enjoy the success as the first mover.

For example, Wal-Mart has conservatively spent 10 times what Amazon.com has to catch up and ask yourself: when was the last time you bought something at walmart.com vs. Amazon.com?

Likewise, other industries, such as the travel industry and the stock brokerage industry, ignored the Internet at their peril. Ask yourself this question: when was the last time you called a travel agent to make a plane (or hotel) reservation vs. just booking it online? Likewise, for those of you that own stocks, when was the last time you called a broker to trade stocks vs. going online?

Hundreds of billions of dollars in wealth were created during the Internet revolution and here's the punch line: <u>the mobile revolution is estimated to be at least 5 times larger</u>.

Remember: by the year 2013, more users will access the Internet from a mobile device than from a desktop computer.

The only question is who will get there first: you or your competitors? Reread the paragraph above about the first mover's advantage with Amazon.com and how much money Walmart has spent to <u>try</u> to catch up. Then ask yourself again: can you really afford to wait?

Mobile Marketing Success: Case Studies

O ne of best ways to see how a new technology can be used to is to study how other companies have done it. This chapter shares how Fortune 500 companies and small businesses have succeed with mobile marketing. Note that not every company featured here was interested in just growing sales: some were interested in increasing brand awareness while some were interested in improving customer loyalty.

As you read through these case studies, be clear on what your objectives are. Please note that some of the technologies mentioned may not be familiar to you at the moment, and these will be further explained throughout the book.

Industry: Restaurant chain
Company profiled: Pappa John's
Technologies used: Mobile texting
Objective: Pappa John's wanted to offer convenience to its consumers by offering the ability to order pizzas from mobile phones. Within 6 months of implementation, the company brought in a reported $1 million of sales, and 20% of sales are now coming from mobile phones.

Industry: News and non-profits
Company profiled: CNN
Technologies used: QR codes
Objective: The recent Japan earthquake disaster helped showcase how QR codes can help raise awareness of a global issue and also increase donations for Japan. During CNN's coverage of the recent disaster, they had a QR code that enabled viewers to scan in and be taken to a site with legitimate charities.

Industry: Retail
Company profiled: Furniture chain

Technologies used: Mobile coupons
Objective: The chain wanted to stimulated sales during a slow period and sent out 6,000 text message coupons to a list who has requested to be notified of VIP offers. The coupons alerted the recipients of a secret sale, and the retailer credited 70% of the sale to the mobile text coupons with every dollar spent on the text campaign generating $100 in revenues.

Industry: Restaurant
Company profiled: Subway franchisee
Technologies used: Mobile coupons
Objective: One of the multi-unit franchisees wanted to expand its customer base and generate more business. To kickstart the effort, the franchisee advertises the campaign via brochure, radio and TV advertising. The consumers were encouraged to register to receive a coupon, and according to the franchisee, text messages sent out to the 5000-plus recipients result in "near instant customer traffic."

Industry: Coffee Chain
Company profiled: Starbucks Mexico
Technology used: QR codes
Objective: To drive additional sales and build loyalty, Starbucks Mexico rolled out a campaign where consumers can receive a QR bar code by texting in. The offer changed each time the bar code was scanned, thus encouraging repeat visits. Starbucks Mexico experienced a 60% redemption rate on the first redemption (the redemption rate for coupons is typically in the 10% range).

Industry: Fashion
Company profiled: Armani Exchange
Technologies used: Mobile advertising

Objective: Armani Exchange wanted to increase awareness, grow its list of prospects and build a stronger connection to the brand with its target audience of 18-49 year olds, a very desirable affluent market segment. With that in mind, the company launched a mobile advertising campaign with a custom mobile site that resulted in 48,000 visits to its mobile site and 2,600 store locator look-ups.

Industry: Automobile
Company profiled: BMW Germany
Technologies used: Mobile texting
Objective: To sell more tires, BMW Germany sent customized mobile text messages to a database that had previously registered to be notified of offers. The message was tailored with a personalized greeting, recommended a specific tire for the car, gave the price and listed the dealerships in the area of the recipient. The campaign achieved a 30% conversion rate, undoubtedly due its personalized nature.

Industry: Airline
Company profiled: Northwest Airlines (NWA)
Technologies used: QR codes
Objective: NWA's objective was to position itself as a technology thought leader and also collect contact email data for its target market. With that in mind, NWA added QR codes to a wide variety of outdoor media including billboards, posters and coin lockers. Scanning the QR took the user to a site built specifically for this campaign. The campaign generated a huge amount of PR and 16,000 hits to its destination site, a 35% increase over the targeted goals.

Defining Your Mobile Marketing Plan

*M*arketing, at its core, is about communication and engagement. As a business owner and a marketer, your goal should be to:

- Communicate the benefits of your product or service to your prospects to get them to buy from you

- Deliver value to your customers that have bought from you to continue buying from you

- Wow your customers so they provide referrals to you.

In defining your mobile marketing plan, your overall goals may include one of the following:

- Generating additional leads and marketing to them – an example of this is adding QR codes to your existing marketing that can add leads to your database: once these leads have been added, you can then market to them in a variety of ways (the most common is text marketing)

- Increasing additional revenues from your existing customer base – the easiest sale to make is to an existing customers, and mobile marketing allows you to provide special promotions in a timely and cost-effective manner

- Improving your customer loyalty to reduce customer churn – in almost every business, the biggest expensive is the customer acquisition cost. In those businesses, simply reducing the customer turnover can dramatically improve profits, and mobile marketing can help accomplish that

- Engaging your audience through interactive promotions – one of the key strengths of mobile marketing is that it's interactive. That is, you can create promotions that solicit customer feedback: an example of this would be a restaurant that surveys its list to find out which soup flavor the restaurant should add to the menu

- Increasing brand awareness –in industries that have long sale cycles (such as real estate), being at the forefront of the front buyer's (or seller's) mind when a buying (or selling) decision is made can mean the difference between having a profitable or unprofitable month

- Stimulating word of mouth (WOM) marketing– WOM marketing often depends on the ability for the WOM source to easily pass along the message, and a mobile message (text or even video) is very easy to pass along

- Improving the user experience – a recent study by Morgan Stanley shows that approximately 25% of Internet browsing now happens from a mobile device and by the year 2013, more people will browse the Internet from a mobile device than from a desktop. Unfortunately, another study shows that over 97% of web sites are not mobile friendly – in some cases, this is an inconvenience and in many other cases, the site is completely unusable. By making your site mobile friendly, you are demonstrating to your prospects and customers that you understand that their needs are evolving

- Educating your prospects to increase their buying confidence – one of the most powerful use of mobile marketing is the QR code, which can provide additional information about your firm or products. By making this information easily accessible to your prospects, this can increase their confidence in their buying decision.

-

In defining your mobile marketing plan, here are the key investments you need to be aware of:

Investment	Description
Strategy development	A commonly overlooked step is defining the strategy of how mobile marketing should be integrated with your existing marketing – this also referred to as the discovery process. Unless you have done this before, it is recommended that you engage a mobile consultant since there are many pitfalls
Implementation	This is the implementation of the strategy after it has been defined
Conversion	By default, sites are

	designed to be viewed on a computer browser and in order to make a site mobile friendly, there has to be a conversion process
Content licensing	These fees include licensing fees or design fees for any content you may use for campaign such as images, videos, etc.
Technologies	Key technologies include the messaging platform and hosting fees (avoid developing something in-house since that can get very expensive very quickly: instead, work with a solutions provider who has already absorbed the cost of licensing the technologies)
Transactional items	The most common example of this is the text credits used during text marketing
Traditional media integration	This refers to the additional investment required to jumpstart your mobile marketing efforts such as adding a QR code to your storefront or existing marketing materials

Before embarking on a major initiative, it's highly recommended that you start with a pilot project.

A pilot project could be starting with text messaging to drive time-sensitive offers, evolve to add QR codes to add new prospects (remember to make your web site friendly if the action from the QR scan is to take the person to the web site).

To see how we can help see, go to page 61 to schedule a 20 minute consultation ($297 value) for FREE.

Personal Notes:

Getting Customers with Text Marketing

*H*ow would you like a marketing channel that guarantees almost instant delivery, has an open rate of 97%, is interactive and can be done for pennies per message? In fact, this marketing channel is so addictive that states have now passed laws from engaging with it because it has increased accidents on the road?

This is not fantasy: it already exists and it's the most basic form of mobile marketing. We are referring to text marketing also referred to as SMS (short message service).

Here are some statistics that may stagger you:

- In a recent American Idol (for those of you outside the US, this is a popular talent show where the audience texts in which candidates should win to go to the next round), the audience texted in a record breaking 78 million text messages during a single episode! It's been estimated that American Idol generates hundreds of millions annually from the markup on text messages (each incoming text is charged to the texter, and American Idol splits this revenue with the carrier)

- 62% of cell phone usage is for sending text messages

- By 2012, it's estimated that over 10 trillion text messages will be delivered (the average teen sends 2,272 messages per month: remember, the teen today is your consumer tomorrow)

- 97% of text messages are opened and 83% of them are opened within an hour (by comparison, the open rate of an email is about 10% in most industries, and this number continues to decline)

- There are over 4.5 billion cell phones worldwide and all of these phones can receive text messages (contrast this with QR codes which require a smart phone: see the section on QR code for more information). There's an emerging standard known as Multimedia Messaging Service (MMS) which even allows you to include images, audio and even video clips. Imagine the power of being able to send a video clip with a special offer or a welcome message to a new customer

At the core of text marketing is a 6 digit Common Short Code (CSC) often referred to as the "short code": this number is assigned to you by the technology vendor or the team responsible for your implementation.

You then instruct your prospects or your customers to text in a phrase (known as the "keyword"). The act of texting to your short code adds the consumer to your list, and this process is often referred to as opting in. The Mobile Marketing Association prohibits companies from sending messages to consumers unless they opt-in so make sure you follow this step. Likewise, every outbound message you send should include a way for the consumer to opt out from receiving any more messages.

We recommend you use a separate keyword per campaign or promotion. For example, if you're a restaurant, you may have 2 different campaigns, one for weekly specials (the keyword may be "weekly" and one for one-off offers (such as "2for1"). You can then allow your patrons to select which campaigns they want to be notified of (one or both). This demonstrates a key benefit of text marketing which is the ability to tailor your messages based on your consumer's preference.

The number of ways that you can use text marketing to get customers is limited only by your imagination but here are some examples to stimulate your imagination:

Industry	Possible Uses
Accountants	<ul><li>Remind clients that their returns are ready to be picked up</li><li>Remind clients to come in for their quarterly planning meetings</li><li>Send an electronic thank you text after the visit and reward the patient for repeat visits and/or referrals</li></ul>
Auto repair shops	<ul><li>Remind the car owners that their cars are ready</li><li>Remind car owners of regular tune-ups</li><li>Notify patrons of seasonal promotions</li></ul>

	• Send an electronic thank you text after the visit and reward the patient for repeat visits and/or referrals
Beauty salons / spas	• Remind patrons of their regular grooming schedule • Notify patrons of seasonal promotions
Churches	• Send out reminders to encourage service attendance • Send out surveys to encourage more interactivity with the congregation
Health clubs	• Remind clients of their appointments with personal trainers • Notify patrons of seals promotions (bring a friend, family plan, etc.)
Lawyers	• Remind clients of their appointments • Remind clients of regular update to legal paperwork (estate

	planning, wills, etc.)
Nightclubs and bars	• Send coupons in a timely manner • Create a VIP clientele by sending out secret codes • Send an electronic thank you text after the visit and reward the customers for repeat visits and/or referrals • Enable customers to text to the screens to increase interactivity and excitement • Send a short video to your prospects to show how "hot" your establishment is and what they are missing out on
Non profits	• Send out reminders about donation drives • Send out messages to build a relationship to encourage donations
Physicians (doctor, chiropractor, dentists, etc.)	• Remind patients of their appointments

	• Remind patients of regular visits • Send an electronic thank you text after the visit and reward the patient for repeat visits and/or referrals
Realtors	• Notify a buyer when a house that matches their needs is available • Notify a seller that a potential buyer is coming by to view the house • Send a series of messages to stay in front of the buyer or seller throughout the long buying/selling process • Send a short video message to the buyer to engage them before they come to the property
Retail stores	• Send coupons in a timely manner • Create a VIP clientele

	by sending out secret codes • Send an electronic thank you text after the visit and reward the patient for repeat visits and/or referrals
Restaurants	• Send coupons in a timely manner • Create a VIP clientele by sending out secret codes • Survey the patrons to see what new dishes to add to the menu • Send an electronic thank you text after the visit and reward the patient for repeat visits and/or referrals

Even with this extensive list, this barely scratches the tip of what's possible. As we mentioned, you are only limited by your imagination and the technology you adopt. Note that not all the features mentioned above are available on all mobile platforms.

For more case studies, see the section of the same name.

To create your own success story, go to page 61 to schedule a 20 minute consultation ($297 value) for FREE.

Getting Customers with QR Codes

QR codes stand for "Quick Response" codes and allow you to broaden your interaction with your clients in some pretty amazing ways.

These 2 dimensional bar codes are the big brother of the regular bar codes you commonly see printed on most consumer products. Regular bar codes are used to uniquely identify products and when they interact with software at the super market checkout the help identify the price, inventory levels, etc.

QR codes on the other hand can store much more information and their interaction with mobile devices makes them a very nifty tool for all kind of businesses.

While very popular in Japan and other countries, smart phone users in the US are just discovering all the things they can learn from QR codes, but they are adopting this "new" technology at a very fast pace because of all the benefits it provides them.

QR codes allow you to share all kinds of content with your buyers and prospects such as contact details, events, a Google maps location, additional product information, links to videos, etc.

In essence, QR codes have become a very easy to use and come in handy when narrowing the bridge between the physical world and the digital world.

How many times have you written down a URL you saw during the day to go find it online when you get home? Do you even remember to do it? QR codes solve the problem by serving the content instantly right in the user's hand upon scanning the code, thus providing instant gratification to their curiosity and an extra opportunity for you to generate additional sales.

QR codes make for great conversation pieces and can be printed creatively on almost anything you'd like, from common things like business cards or magazine ads to things like store front signs, t-shirts, hats or even temporary tattoos.

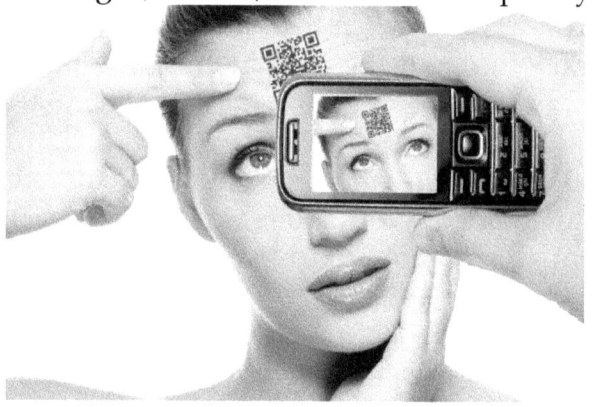

Because of their versatility you are only limited by your imagination and creativity on how you can use QR codes to better market your business and interact with your customers.

Here are some ways to use a QR code to ramp up your sales and create customer interaction with your business:

In store front signs or windows: If you are a restaurant you could have the QR code display your menu, prices or maybe the special of the day, even a welcome video from you or your chef, inviting patrons inside for a special treat. Retail outlets can provide more information on a specific product being displayed, a secret deal of the day video or even create an online contest that would catch the attention of more customers.

In your marketing materials: if you are producing any kind of printed materials like flyers, brochures, and business cards. You can add a QR code to show your prospect photos, a video interview or maybe even interactively answer frequently asked questions.

At events: You can use QR codes on your ID badge to exchange your business information (vcard) or use them on the schedule to guide attendees to specific events (vcalendar). Briefs or bios of the speakers can also be linked to from the QR code giving the attendees all the information they need right in their hand.

No matter how you use QR codes you must remember that not everyone is familiar with them, so it is a good idea to invite users to the interaction with a simple "Scan here for smart phone interaction" or invite them to interact with a "Scan code for 10% off their purchase" or "Scan here for a Free Side order" and make sure your employees know how to scan them so they can help any customer with questions.

Here are a few examples of how companies of all types are embracing this new technology:

- The New York Department of Sanitation are featuring QR codes on 2,200 NYC sanitation trucks linking to a "How to Recycle" video created by Hocast

- Calvin Klein used a giant QR code in their "Get It Uncensored" campaign that when scanned took you to a "racy" movie

As you can see QR codes are becoming more popular by the day and you are only limited by your imagination on how to put them to use.

To get your creative juices flowing here is a list of things you can encode in your QR code.

- Any type of text

- Your website address
- Your phone number
- An SMS message
- Your email address
- An email message
- Your contact details (vcard)
- Event details (vcalendar)
- Google Maps location
- PayPal's "Buy Now" link
- Social media pages or "likes"
- iTunes link
- YouTube video
- And much, much more

Getting Customers with Mobile Websites

*7*he short term growth of mobile online shopping has been jaw dropping. In the United States alone, mobile online shopping has grown from 396.3 million in 2008 to over $3.4 billion in 2010 (this isn't counting travel related purchases (plane, hotel, etc.), which adds another $1.5 billion.

DotMobi, the mobile Web solution provider behind the .mobi extension, announced in its October 2010 study that that the two year global mobile content growth outpaces growth of the desktop Web in the equivalent period.

But even with such an accelerated growth, most businesses aren't ready for this influx of customers. DotMobi's study revealed that from Alexa's (the Amazon.com analytics company) top 500,000 sites online, less than 20% are mobile friendly making them slower and in most cases hard to read.

57% **OF ONLINE CONSUMERS** will abandon a site after waiting **3 seconds** for a page to load.

80% of these people **WILL NOT RETURN.**

Of these... **Almost half will go on to tell others about their negative experience.**

Web pages are bigger and more complex than ever and if you don't have their mobile ready counterpart, they will render slowly to the end user and most likely it will be displayed incorrectly too.

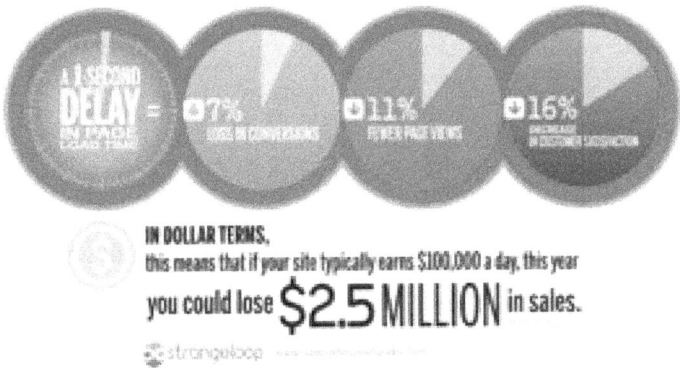

As a study realized by Forrester Research on behalf or Akamai reveals the impact of Poor Performing Sites:

- 79% of dissatisfied shoppers are less likely to buy from an online site again
- 75% would be less likely to even return to the website again
- 61% of online shoppers who spend more than $1,500 online per year insist on pages loading quickly
- After a poor site experience, 27% are less likely to buy from that retailer OFFLINE!

To properly build a mobile website you must take several factors into consideration:

- It must properly identify the device that's being used to deliver the proper page to the end user. This could be a specific page size for a mobile phone brand or the regular page to someone browsing from a computer

- You must prepare your content for your mobile site. Mobile users don't have the time or patience to read your full site content. Pick out the most relevant information you want to present them
- Your design should be light and not use many images or pictures because of the slower bandwidth of a mobile device
- Your mobile site should provide easy and intuitive navigation. Try not to have some complex navigation system where the users have to guess what to click to find what they're looking for
- Along with the right content you should structure it in a way that it all important information is only or two clicks away
- Make sure all the links you use in your site are pointing only to other mobile optimized pages, you don't want to send a mobile user to a non-

optimized page and immediately lose them

- Mobile sites are best displayed in a one column display with sliding menus to keep everything well organized. The extra work it takes to make this special layout will be well worth the trouble

After creating your mobile website, you will still have to invest to bring visitors to the site so it gets views and you can generate more sales. To do this, you can combine multiple techniques as text messages, QR codes, social media, etc.

Soon the number of mobile internet users will surpass the desktop Internet users.

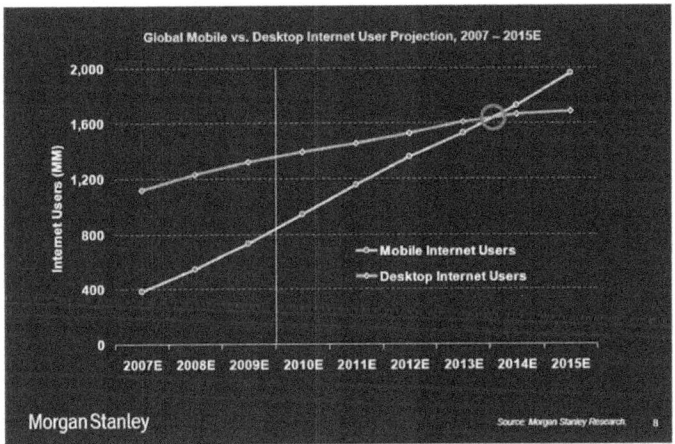

If you don't start preparing a mobile marketing plan to serve all these users, you'll probably be left behind and your current website will bring in even less customers than it does today.

Getting More Customers with Social Media

*D*iscussing mobile marketing without social media would be incomplete since 47% of mobile users browse social media sites on their mobile devices. Social media has been a hot topic for the past couple of years and it doesn't seem it will be cooling down any time soon. Facebook now has over 500 million users worldwide and Twitter is about to reach 300 million users. The investor market has also paid attention because Twitter has been valued at $10 billion, and Facebook has been valued at over $50 billion (approximately ¼ the valuation of Microsoft).

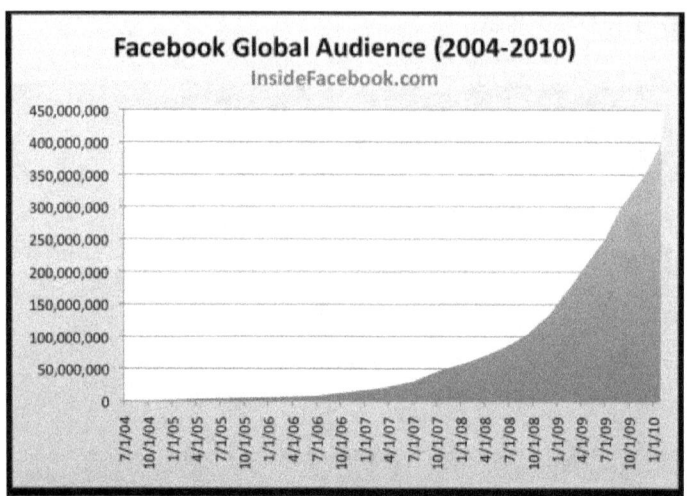

No matter what you think about social media, be it a great opportunity or just a waste of time, it's an undeniable fact that social media enables companies to listen and communicate with their customers directly and as frequently as necessary.

Businesses who embrace social media are able to build strong relationships with their customers and reach new frontiers of customer service.

Marketing is no longer a one way road. In today's world, customers are engaged with conversations about our products and services, some are intended for us to hear and some aren't, so you better pay attention and listen to what they are saying in order to serve them better. Your competitors are most likely paying attention to these conversations too and just waiting for the right conversation to start to snap those customers from under your nose.

Currently almost half of small businesses find customers in social networks. This is the result of a study published by Regus, a workplace solution provider, where they surveyed senior managers and business owners around the world.

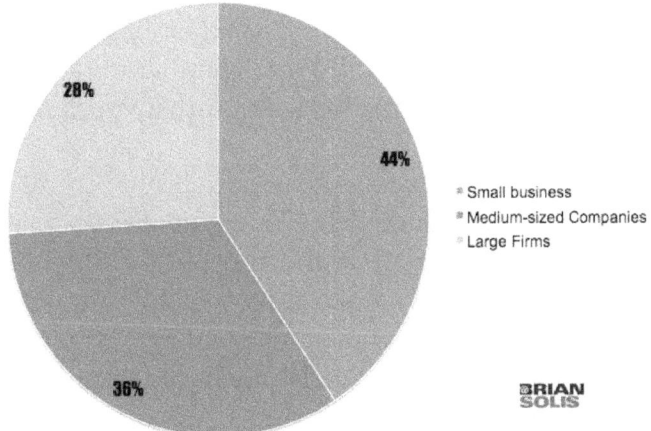

Since this is something we can no longer ignore, it is of vital importance for us to have a well-defined social media strategy to survive in this new "connected" economy.

Not only will a well-defined strategy allow you to get the greatest bang for your busk with social media, but it will also allow you to decide if tackling social media is something you want to do on your own or if you better outsource it.

Up until now social media had been optional for businesses large and small. Some had dipped their toes in and other has been ignoring social media altogether but leading social media expert Charlene Li predicts:

> "Companies that do not get on the social media bandwagon soon–within three to five years–will not survive" – Charlene Li

As shown in an earlier chart small businesses are slower to adopt social media, this is because they mostly lack a web presence at all so it is twice as important for you to start taking corrective actions in the right direction **today**!

It is understandable that this can be a huge and sometimes scary goal to achieve because of all that has to be done to implement it correctly, but that's when you really have to consider hiring a company with enough experience to give you a hand.

A recent research conducted by Constant Contact, a leading email provider, revealed that the most important marketing tactic to acquiring new customers is word of mouth (WOM). WOM is over 20% more important than any other tactic and you must remember that WOM includes both online and offline discussions.

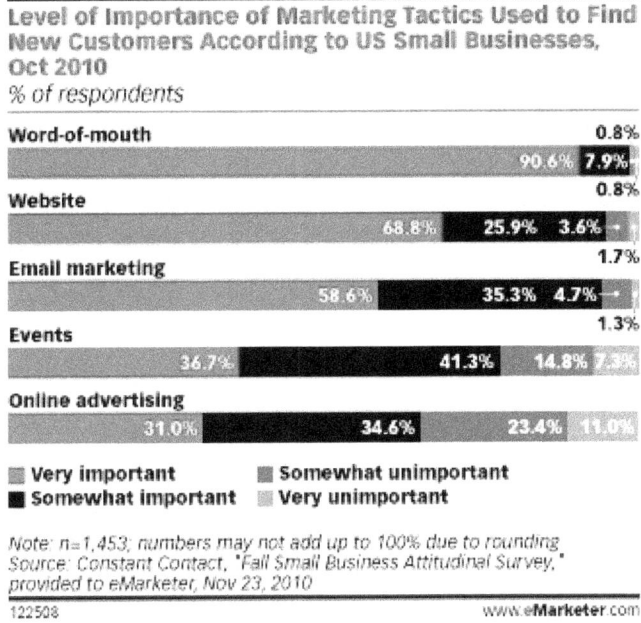

Level of Importance of Marketing Tactics Used to Find New Customers According to US Small Businesses, Oct 2010

% of respondents

| Word-of-mouth | | 0.8% |
| 90.6% | 7.9% | |

| Website | | 0.8% |
| 68.8% | 25.9% | 3.6% |

| Email marketing | | 1.7% |
| 58.6% | 35.3% | 4.7% |

| Events | | 1.3% |
| 36.7% | 41.3% | 14.8% 7.3% |

| Online advertising | | |
| 31.0% | 34.6% | 23.4% 11.0% |

■ Very important   ■ Somewhat unimportant
■ Somewhat important   Very unimportant

Note: n=1,453; numbers may not add up to 100% due to rounding
Source: Constant Contact, "Fall Small Business Attitudinal Survey," provided to eMarketer, Nov 23, 2010

122508   www.eMarketer.com

Social media clearly allows you not only to reach your customers but also to listen to their wants and needs.

It also allows you to spy in on your competition, what their clients are talking about and it provides a way for you to reach out and interact with your competitors customers. But a word of caution…it allows your competitors to do the same thing so you better have a good plan in place.

Getting new customers is not the only thing you can do with social media, it also all to turn your current customers into repeat customers! This can be done by constantly keeping in touch with them, listening to their needs and offering them what they're looking for.

The best way to keep in touch with your current customers is to direct them and engage them on social media sites and help them become your friend, follower or fan. In some cases they'll be glad to become your friend and follow you, but in other cases you have to be creative and bribe them (or incentivize them if you prefer this word) to get them to connect with you.

A simple way to incentivize a customer is through coupons or special offers that are only available for those who like follow, fan, etc. Don't stop at the first gift: keep the offers coming so your customers come back over and over again.

A good starting point for your social media plan is decide on which sites you will focus on, and begins building a community through simple conversations, and offers.

- There is no doubt that Facebook should be one of these sites. With over 500 million registered users, Facebook is a great place to learn from your audiences

- Twitter effectively spreads your message among people who are interested in what you want to say. Also its search capabilities is the perfect tool to listen to your customers conversations

- YouTube is a great way to leverage the video content you are creating. Recently, Google (who owns YouTube) has added many social aspects to YouTube which are working fabulously

- There are also social sites for your pictures, presentations, and bookmarks and almost for any kind of content you create. Even if the interaction with these isn't that frequent you must take them into consideration

A couple other social sites that are very well oriented in getting more customers are:

- Foursquare – Foursquare really does a good job in spreading the word and also allows you to use creative ways to incentivize customers to come to your business
- Yelp – Yelp is the voice of the customer but allows you to step in and find out how they are specifically talking about your products and services

New social media sites pop up every week and obviously others die, and that's why sometimes it's hard to decide in which ones you should participate in. This is where working with a proven team can really come in handy.

As you can see, there are many moving pieces to a social media strategy and even though it is complicated you must dive into it as soon as possible to not be left behind.

Should You Outsource?

*W*hen rolling out your mobile marketing campaigns, a key decision is to determine whether to use your own resources internally or outsource it to a team that specializes in mobile marketing campaigns.

The table below can help you to determine whether to outsource your mobile marketing campaigns or not.

Questions	Score
Have you ever implemented a mobile marketing campaign? Rolling out a mobile project is a complex effort and it's nearly impossible to execute without prior experience. In many cases, business owners engage us to manage the effort because we can create and identify additional revenue streams and implement strategies to monetize these income streams.	• Minus 5 points if you have not implemented at least one mobile marketing campaign and you intend on winging it • Add 0 points if you haven't done a mobile marketing campaign and you know you need help • Add 5 points if you have implemented a mobile campaign already

Do you have an existing dedicated project manager (PM) on your staff with mobile marketing experience? A mobile marketing campaign requires expertise and dedicated staff. A key role in such an effort is a project manager (PM) whose only responsibility is the success of the project. Many clients we have worked with lack a project manager role, (the office manager usually plays that role) and in the rare cases that there is a project manager, he doesn't have hands-on mobile marketing experience.	• Minus 5 points if you don't even have a project manager role defined • Add 0 points if you have identified the role but don't have that role filled • Add 1 point if you currently have a dedicated Project manager but with no mobile marketing experience • Add 5 points if that project manager has mobile marketing experience
Do you have a dedicated technical architect? Most clients we have worked with seriously underestimate all the technical issues that need to be addressed on a	• Minus 5 points if you don't even have a technical architect

daily basis and these issues are even worse during the rollout of a mobile marketing campaign due to all the technologies that are required to make things work. All of these issues are best handled by a technical architect (TA). Even if you outsource most of your technologies, you need somebody on staff who understands the compromises that are made with every technical decision that is being made (you always make compromises when working with technologies, whether you realize it or not). If you make a couple of key mistakes here (such as picking the wrong hosting company or the wrong mobile platform), your campaign is practically guaranteed to fail.	role defined • Add 0 points if you have identified the role but don't have that role filled • Add 1 point if you currently have a dedicated technical architect but has no mobile marketing experience • Add 5 points if that technical architect has mobile marketing experience (which is significantly different than day to day operational experience)
Do you have a marketing strategy? Mobile marketing	• Minus 5 points if you don't have a

shouldn't be your total solution: it should be part of an overall marketing plan that is designed to generate sales.	marketing strategy • Add 5 points if you have a marketing strategy

Here is your scoring table to help you determine your course of action:

Questions	Score
-20 to 5	You're in over your head. Outsource immediately or you risk your whole campaign blowing up.
5 to 10	You have textbook knowledge but still lack hands-on experience.
11 to 15	You are qualified to do a pilot project, but expect to run into some pitfalls.
15 to 20	You can definitely still benefit from outside help because you are probably overlooking some key income streams.
21 to 25	You're ready for rolling out a mobile marketing campaign, but you may still want to get outside help for execution.

Special $297 Offer For FREE

(Only For Readers of This Book)

We wrote this book to provide you an overview of what mobile marketing is and how it can be used to grow your business. We know that you probably still have questions such as:

- Is my business ready for mobile marketing?

- What are some pitfalls I need to know before adopting mobile marketing and/or social media?

- Which of the many mobile marketing methods are appropriate for my business?

That is natural and we want to offer you an opportunity to have a 20 minute mobile strategy session with us. We normally charge $3,000 per day individually for consulting (and the clients come to us), and what you will discover during the 20 minutes is worth way more than the $297 we normally charge for this.

To book your mobile strategy session with us simply email me at info@SMPForMe.com and request a 1 on 1 consulting. Just mention this book and we will then contact within 72 hours. Or just call us at 678-318-1888

Please be patient with us because we have a very long queue for our services, and we're very selective about who we offer our services to. After all, your success is our success.

Your Next Steps

There's a great Zen saying: "The journey is the reward." That captures the entire essence of the mobile market: it is a living, breathing thing and is constantly evolving. Your next steps depend on where you are.

If you are already doing mobile marketing – and congratulations because you're in the very small minority – then use these strategies to magnify your income.

*If you haven't integrated mobile marketing into your business, then get ready for the best ride of your life. You will be pleasantly surprised at how fast a mobile campaign can add profits to your bottom line. Read the section, "**Special $297 Offer For FREE (Only for Readers of This Book)**" and book your complimentary 1-1 mobile strategy session with us.*

To bigger profits,

- Rateb "Rock" Shukoor -

Contact Information

Contact Rock Shukoor at:

Website: www.SMPForMe.com
And www.RockTheInvestor.com

Email: info@SMPForMe.com

Benefits that we can deliver to you include:
- Creating a roadmap that explains how to integrate mobile marketing and social media with your other marketing efforts
- Adding new **customers** with mobile marketing and social media
- Increasing brand loyalty with mobile marketing and social media
- Stimulating more sales from your existing customers
- Creating a buzz and increasing more word of mouth referrals
- Implementing the right technologies to ensure accurate tracking of your mobile and other campaigns
- And much, much more

Schedule your complimentary 20 minute mobile marketing strategy session by sending us an email at info@SMPForMe.com of simply calling us at 678-318-1888 (for more information, see the "**Special $297 Offer For FREE (Only for Readers of This Book)**" section.

This book is dedicated to:

My loving family, what would I ever do without you? You are the greatest support system anyone could ever wish to have and I am 'blessed' to have you in my life. Thank you for cheering me on and supporting me in my passion. Thank you for being a part of my dreams that have come true.

To my "Dream Team", I call you 'guys' my dream team because you make my dreams come true. 'Lone rangers' do not know what they are missing, until they start working with people like you, let them be. I do not want to be one of them, and I would not know how to run a business without the help of knowledgeable and valuable people like you. So, thank you for your help, support and putting up with me through everything. From the deepest crevices of my heart, I sincerely thank you all!

Indeed, this treasure chest of a book could not be possible if not for **All of You.**

- Rateb "Rock" Shukoor –

www.ingramcontent.com/pod-product-compliance
Lightning Source LLC
Chambersburg PA
CBHW071825170526
45167CB00003B/1427